A
WISE
MAN
ONCE
SAID

Timeless Wisdom for Men of All Ages and Stages

JOE L. GIBBONS

FOREWORD BY DARIUS J. WILLIS

River of Life
PUBLISHING

All Scripture quotations are taken from the King James Version (KJV) of the Bible, which is in the public domain.

This book is a work of inspiration and wisdom. Any references to people, places, or events are made respectfully and are intended to uplift and encourage the reader in their spiritual walk.

Printed in the United States of America

ISBN: 978-1-968644-00-0
eBook ISBN: 978-1-968644-01-7
Hardcover ISBN: 978-1-968644-05-5
Library of Congress Control Number: 2025917891

River of Life Publishing
Memphis, Tennessee

Dedication

———— ⚜ ————

This book is lovingly dedicated to my dear wife of over 65 years, Mable Brown Gibbons, whose love, strength, and faith have been the foundation of our family and my greatest earthly blessing.

To my beloved children and their spouses—you are my pride and joy:

- Robin Sonya Willis
- (Bishop James M. Willis)
- Charlotte Denise "Neci" Russell
- (Michael L. Russell, Sr.)
- Keith Fitzgerald Gibbons
- (Nancy Gibbons)
- Karen Francine Hatcher
- (Bishop Gabriel J. Hatcher, Sr.)
- Sharon Annette Gibbons

To my treasured 22 grandchildren and 30 great-grandchildren—you are my heart and my legacy.

May these words guide and bless you for generations to come.

In loving memory of my parents, Joe Gibbons and Queen Ester Gibbons, whose legacy of love and faith shaped the man I became.

To my dear siblings—the late Earnest F. Gibbons, Gladys Gibbons Koger, and David P. Gibbons—your love, support, and presence have been a blessing in my life, and I thank God for each of you.

Contents

Dedication

Acknowledgments

Foreword

Preface

Acknowledgments

First, I give thanks and glory to my Lord and Savior, Jesus Christ, who has kept me through all these years. I also honor the Holy Ghost, the Spirit of wisdom, who has been my source of understanding—guiding me into all truth and helping me make wise decisions day by day.

I thank God for the Word of God—the Holy Bible—which has been my guide and anchor in every season.

I acknowledge with gratitude my pastor of over 50 years, the late Bishop Charles D. Williams, and Mother Fannie Mae Williams, whose teaching and example helped shape my spiritual walk.

I also extend thanks to my current pastor, Bishop Otis McCormick, and Mother Arlene McCormick for their continued leadership, prayers, and support.

I honor the late Mother Ira Lee Cotton—a woman of great wisdom, a pillar in my life and in my family's life. Her impact still echoes through the generations.

To some of my dearest and closest friends, the late Elder Elbert Hawk and Mother Oneatha K. Hawk—your friendship and fellowship were blessings beyond words.

To my church family, Greater Friendly Temple Church Of God In Christ—you have been my home, joy, and community.

I also want to acknowledge and thank all those who helped my grandson, Darius J. Willis, as he compiled this book: my beloved wife, Mable Gibbons, whose love has been constant; my granddaughter, Dorena Willis, who stood as her brother's right hand; my daughters, Robin Willis, Karen Hatcher, and Neci Russell; my granddaughter, Yolanda Gibbons; my brother, David Gibbons; my sister, Gladys Kroger; and my niece, Theresa Woods—all of you played a part. The wisdom I've shared with you over the years has come full circle, and I'm grateful for your hands, hearts, and help in bringing this vision to life.

Finally, to all who have walked this journey with me, prayed for me, and encouraged me—I am grateful beyond measure.

Foreword

━━━━━━━━━━━━━━━━━━ ⚜ ━━━━━━━━━━━━━━━━━━

My grandfather, Joe L. Gibbons, is one of the wisest men I have ever known. Throughout my life, I have watched him walk with humility, patience, and a quiet strength that speaks louder than words. His wisdom does not come from books or degrees, but from a deep well of experience, hard work, and most importantly, his unwavering faith in God.

He is a godly man: a man of prayer, a man of the Word, and a man whose life has been shaped by seeking God's guidance in all things. As a husband, father, grandfather, great-grandfather, and friend, he has shown what it truly means to love, lead, and serve. His love for our family is unmatched, and his example has been a steady light for all of us who follow in his footsteps.

James 1:5-6 says, "If any of you lack wisdom, let him ask of God, that giveth to all men liberally, and upbraideth not; and it shall be given him. But let him ask in faith, nothing wavering."

My grandfather is a living testimony of this verse. He is a man who has consistently asked God for wisdom and walked it out in faith without wavering.

Proverbs 4:7 teaches us, "Wisdom is the principal thing; therefore get wisdom: and with all thy getting get understanding."

The pursuit of wisdom has been the foundation of my grandfather's life. He has inclined his ear to wisdom (Proverbs 2:2), sought understanding, and applied the knowledge given by God (Proverbs 2:6). He has not only gained wisdom, but he has also lived it, and now he is passing it on.

As you read the pages of this book, you are not just reading quotes and reflections. Know you are receiving treasures—timeless truths forged in the fires of life and faith. These nuggets of wisdom have been lived, tested, and proven over ninety years. They are not just words on paper—they are treasures from a life well lived, the result of prayer, reflection, and a lifetime of listening to God.

Scripture tells us, "My son, hear the instruction of thy father, and forsake not the law of thy mother: For they shall be an ornament of grace unto thy head"

(Proverbs 1:8-9). My grandfather has fulfilled that scripture, offering instruction with grace, truth, and humility. He has remembered the days of old and shared them with us, just as Deuteronomy 32:7 commands: "Ask thy father, and he will shew thee; thy elders, and they will tell thee."

He has taught us that wisdom is greater than wealth: "How much better is it to get wisdom than gold! and to get understanding rather to be chosen than silver!" (Proverbs 16:16). And in a world filled with noise and distraction, his life reminds us that "wisdom giveth life to them that have it" (Ecclesiastes 7:12).

Psalm 78:3-4 declares, "Which we have heard and known, and our fathers have told us. We will not hide them from their children." This book is a fulfillment of that charge. It is a living legacy—wisdom passed from one generation to the next.

Proverbs 13:20 tells us, "He that walketh with wise men shall be wise." As you journey through the pages of this book, you are walking with a wise man. And if you listen closely, you'll find strength, truth, and clarity for your own path.

It has been my honor and joy to help bring these nuggets together so they can bless you as they have blessed our family. May you find encouragement, direction, and wisdom for every stage of your life in this book. And may you, like my grandfather, walk in faith and trust in the God who gives wisdom generously to all who ask.

— *Darius J. Willis*
Grandson & Editor

Preface

W hen we think of wisdom, we often imagine scholars, leaders, or philosophers. But sometimes, the deepest wisdom is found in the everyday life of someone who has quietly lived with integrity, love, and faith. Elder Joe L. Gibbons, at ninety years old, is such a man—a living wellspring of wisdom for his family, friends, church, and community.

Elder Gibbons never set out to write a book. However, over time, his family began collecting the nuggets of wisdom he shared—words offered at family gatherings, quiet conversations, church meetings, and countless moments in between. We realized these words were too valuable to keep to ourselves. They have shaped our lives in quiet but powerful ways.

That's why we put this book together—to create a space where others could sit with his wisdom, just like we have. This is not just a record of thoughts—it's a living legacy. It is our family's gift to you, a way to share the heart of a godly man whose life has touched many.

"With the ancient is wisdom; and in length of days understanding" (Job 12:12 KJV).

Introduction

—————————— ⚜ ——————————

This book is a heartfelt collection of wisdom gathered over a lifetime by Elder Joe L. Gibbons—a devoted husband, father, grandfather, great-grandfather, and servant of God. Although Elder Gibbons never set out to write a book, his family recognized the deep reservoir of wisdom he has shared over the years that has shaped generations and continues to touch lives today.

At every stage of life, a man encounters challenges, joys, and decisions that define his journey. What does it mean to be a wise son, brother, husband, father, grandfather, or leader? How should one carry oneself when young, married, working, or retired?

In *A Wise Man Once Said*, Joe Gibbons offers simple yet profound wisdom for men in every age and stage of life. These pages contain practical insights, spiritual encouragement, and godly advice, lovingly compiled by his family to bless all who read them. We knew we could not keep these powerful truths to ourselves. They offer meaning and hope to any man seeking guidance and encouragement.

As you turn these pages, you will find reflections shaped by a lifetime of faith, hard work, and love. Whether you are a young man just starting out, a husband striving to love well, a grandfather seeking to leave a godly legacy, or a preacher or church leader shepherding others, there is something here for you.

Each chapter also provides space for your reflections and personal insights—lessons learned or passed down through experience—making this book not just a tribute to Elder Gibbons' wisdom, but a living, growing legacy of your own.

It is our heartfelt prayer that these "nuggets" of wisdom will inspire, strengthen, challenge, and guide you—just as they have done for us.

"A wise man will hear, and will increase learning; and a man of understanding shall attain unto wise counsels" (Proverbs 1:5).

Chapter 1

Wisdom for a Son

Honoring the Lessons of Your Parents
and Building a Strong Foundation

Scripture: "My son, hear the instruction of thy father, and forsake not the law of thy mother" (Proverbs 1:8).

Devotion: As a son, you are a student of life. Do not only learn from books but from the example and guidance of your parents. Their experience is a treasure map. Follow it, and you'll avoid many pitfalls. Today, pause for a moment to listen and appreciate their counsel.

♦ *Honor your parents' wisdom; it will carry you further than your strength ever could.*
Life will teach you lessons, but if you listen, your parents can help you avoid some of the hardest ones. You may not always agree, but one day you'll understand.

- *Your name is a garment—wear it well.*
  A good name can open doors that money can't.

- *Never be so grown that you can't be corrected.*
  A teachable spirit will keep you out of trouble and in God's favor.

- *Don't wait until it's too late to say thank you.*
  Gratitude isn't just polite—it's powerful. Let your parents hear it while they can still smile about it.

- *Ask questions while your parents are still here to answer.*
  Your parents are a library of life experience—don't leave the books unread.

- *Obedience isn't weakness; it's wisdom in seed form.*
  What you sow today, you'll reap tomorrow.

- *Speak respectfully, even when you disagree.*
  Your tone can build bridges or burn them.

- *Carry your parents' name with dignity.*
  Whether it's your last name or their legacy, don't drag it through the mud.

◆ *Help without being asked.*
A good son anticipates the need, not just re-acts to it.

◆ *Don't just visit—be present.*
Put down the phone, look them in the eyes, and share the moment.

◆ *Forgive quickly.*
Your parents aren't perfect and neither are you. Grace runs both ways.

◆ *Give back while you still can.*
The day may come when your parents will need you like you once needed them.

◆ *Remember: how you treat your parents is how your children may treat you.*
Set the example now for the future you're building.

A Son's Prayer

Heavenly Father,
Thank You for the gift of my parents. I'm grateful for the sacrifices they've made, the lessons they've

taught, and the love they've given—sometimes without thanks or rest. Help me to honor them, not just in words but in how I live. Teach me to be patient, to listen more, and to love them with the same grace You show me every day. Strengthen them where they are weak. Encourage them where they may feel tired, and let them see the fruit of their labor in my life. Make me a son they can be proud of and a man who walks in truth and love. In Jesus' name. Amen.

Wisdom Worth Keeping

Wisdom Worth Keeping

Chapter 2

Wisdom for a Brother

Walking in Loyalty, Love, and Accountability

Scripture: "A friend loveth at all times, and a brother is born for adversity" (Proverbs 17:17).

Devotion: Brothers are more than companions; they are life's built-in support system. Whether it's a blood brother or a brother in Christ, stand with him in hard times. Be the brother who brings strength when the storms come.

- *Be the kind of brother who lifts your siblings when they fall.*
  Sometimes your presence, patience, or prayer is exactly what they need to get back up.

- *Family ties are more than blood—they're built with trust, love, and time.*
  Be someone your siblings can count on when the crowd thins out.

- *Don't compete with your siblings—complete one another.*
  Your strengths may balance their weaknesses, and vice versa. That's how family works.

- *Speak the truth, but speak it with grace.*
  The right words, said in the right spirit, can heal old wounds and deepen the bond.

- *Protect your siblings in private and in public.*
  Whether they're in the room or not, stand up for them like a brother should.

- *Apologize first, forgive fast, and love always.*
  Bitterness is a heavy burden—don't pass it down through generations.

- *Help your siblings become who God made them to be.*
  Push them toward purpose, not just comfort.

- *Show up—not just in times of need but also in times of joy.*
  Your presence speaks louder than any advice you could give.

♦ *Celebrate your siblings' success with a full heart.*
Jealousy shrinks a man's spirit; joy expands it.

♦ *Let your life preach what words cannot.*
Be a brother who sets an example worth fol-
lowing—one of faith, strength, and humility.

A Brother's Prayer

Father God,
Thank You for the sacred calling of brotherhood.
Whether to a brother or a sister, help us to be faithful,
loving, and present. Teach us to lead with humility,
speak with wisdom, and serve with compassion. May
we build bridges, not walls, and sow peace in our
families. Strengthen us to be the kind of brothers who
reflect Your love every day. In Jesus' name. Amen.

Wisdom Worth Keeping

_____

_____

_____

_____

_____

_____

_____

_____

_____

_____

_____

_____

_____

_____

_____

_____

_____

_____

_____

_____

_____

_____

Wisdom Worth Keeping

_____
_____
_____
_____
_____
_____
_____
_____
_____
_____
_____
_____
_____
_____
_____
_____
_____
_____
_____
_____
_____
_____
_____
_____

Chapter 3

Wisdom for a Young Man

Choosing the Right Path Early in Life

Scripture: "How can a young man stay on the path of purity? By living according to your word" (Psalm 119:9).

Devotion: Youth is a season of choices. God's Word is your compass when the world offers detours. Spend time in Scripture, set godly goals, and guard your heart now—your future self will thank you.

- ♦ *Build good habits early; they'll become the tracks your life runs on.*
  It's hard to change course once the groove is set, so start right.

- ♦ *Be smarter than a hammer.*
  A hammer only knows how to hit—nothing more. It can't act on its own; someone has to pick it up and give it purpose. You've got more than strength—you've got a mind. Use

it. A brain that's never used is like a tool left in the box—full of potential but doing nothing.

- *Don't hand anyone a bat to beat you over the head with.*
  Guard your words, time, decisions, and reputation. Everything doesn't need to be shared, especially your weaknesses.

- *Find something to collect.*
  Whether it's books, stamps, or wisdom—it'll teach you discipline, attention to detail, and respect for value.

- *Don't spend all you earn.*
  Tuck something away from every dollar— for now, for the future, and to bless someone else. A young man with a savings habit is rare and wise.

- *Have a vision.*
  Without a vision, you'll drift. With it, you'll build. Know where you're going, or you'll follow anyone.

- *Widen your life's path.*
  Engage with different people, experiences,

and perspectives. The broader you make your life path—the more people, ideas, and experiences you engage with—the more opportunity you'll have for growth. Don't stay on a narrow road just because it feels safe. A narrow mind limits a big future.

♦ *Find someone who has already been where you want to go.*
Find someone who has made it from point A to point Z. Everyone who has ever accomplished anything had an example they followed. Learn from their scars and successes. A smart young man listens more than he talks.

♦ *Ask good questions—but not all at once.*
Pace yourself. Ask focused questions and be ready to listen. Wisdom is gained in doses. Take notes. Reflect. Let it sink in before you chase more.

♦ *You can't ride a bike and fly a kite at the same time.*
Neither is hard, but both require focus. It's not about difficulty—it's about attention.

◆ *No one is born wise.*
Every elder learned from someone or something. Wisdom takes more than one mentor, one book, or one sermon—it's the product of a lifetime of learning.

◆ *You need the right tools for the job.*
A paper kite needs string; a plane needs wings. If you want to go far, get equipped.

◆ *What you practice is what you'll become.*
If you don't practice anything, you won't become anything. Excellence takes effort.

◆ *Life is more than a walk.*
How you walk determines how far you go, how fast you get there, and who you are when you arrive.

◆ *Clarity matters.*
Even a positive thing can turn negative if you're unclear. A good thing can be misunderstood if you don't communicate it well. Be clear. Be honest. Be intentional.

- *Rise to something greater.*
  Find a worthwhile standard—a mentor, a Scripture, a legacy—and reach for it with everything you've got.

- *Build on what you learn from others.*
  Don't just listen—apply it. Knowledge unused is just noise. Build with what you've been given.

- *Don't get tangled up with drugs or alcohol.*
  What feels like a shortcut to escape can become a trap that's hard to get out of. Keep your mind clear and your future clean. Don't hand the Devil the keys to your destiny.

- *You don't have to make every mistake to learn.*
  Pay attention to the scars of others. You don't need to go to jail to know it's not where you want to end up. Be wise enough to learn from the hard lessons others have already lived—you don't have to touch the fire to know it burns.

- *Keep your word.*
  Let people know that when you say something, it's as good as done.

- *Find purpose before you chase profit.*
  If you know who you are and why you're here, you won't sell yourself short for a paycheck.

- *You don't need an education to lay down with someone.*
  Desire without wisdom leads to damage and passion without wisdom can lead to regret.

- *Every decision has a consequence.*
  Think long before you act fast.

- *Don't confuse pride with manhood.*
  Real strength knows when to be silent, when to walk away, and when to apologize.

- *Choose your friends carefully.*
  The people you walk with will influence where you go and how far you get.

- *Pray before you move.*
  God sees around corners—trust Him to guide your steps.

- *Respect women, respect elders, and respect yourself.*
  How you treat others is a reflection of what you believe about yourself.

- *If you don't learn how to do it when you don't have to, you won't know what to do when you need to.*
  Preparation in peace equips you for pressure in crisis.

- *Learn to love music.*
  Music can comfort you when you're lonely, lift your spirit when you're low, and fill your heart with joy. It's a language God often uses to reach the soul.

- *Buying a new car brings peace of mind.*
  There's comfort in knowing the car comes with fewer problems and a warranty. When you can afford it, buy new—or stick with reliable dealerships. Don't gamble on your transportation.

- *There are so many ways in the world, everyone can have their own.*
  You may have your way of doing something,

and I may have mine—and that's all right (Joe Gibbons, Sr.).

♦ *You can, if you try.*
A simple truth with lasting power. Don't let doubt stop what effort can accomplish (Queen Esther Gibbons).

A Young Man's Prayer

Father God,
Thank You for the gift of youth and the opportunity to grow in wisdom and strength. I pray for every young man reading these words—give him discernment beyond his years and a heart that leans on You. Help him walk with integrity, choose wisely, and stand strong when life tests him. Let him be a builder of good habits, a seeker of truth, and a doer of Your Word. Surround him with godly mentors, shield him from traps and temptations, and keep his feet on the path of righteousness. May he never forget who he is—and more importantly, whose he is. In Jesus' name. Amen.

Wisdom Worth Keeping

_____

_____

_____

_____

_____

_____

_____

_____

_____

_____

_____

_____

_____

_____

_____

_____

_____

_____

_____

_____

_____

_____

_____

_____

_____

Wisdom Worth Keeping

_____

_____

_____

_____

_____

_____

_____

_____

_____

_____

_____

_____

_____

_____

_____

_____

_____

_____

_____

_____

_____

_____

Chapter 4

Wisdom for a Single Man

Embracing Purpose, Integrity, Preparation,
and Patience in the Waiting Season

Scripture: "But seek first his kingdom and his righteousness, and all these things will be given to you as well" (Matthew 6:33).

Devotion: Singleness is not a waiting room; it's a classroom. Let God shape your character, deepen your trust, and prepare you for what's ahead. Find joy in this season. You are whole in Christ.

- ◆ *Be complete in Christ before you seek completeness in another.*
  A whole man attracts a whole woman. Let God finish His work in you first.

- ◆ *There comes a time when you have to forget where you came from and focus on where you're going.*
  Don't get stuck in old habits, places, or mindsets—your future needs your full attention.

♦ *What you do in private, if you're not careful, you'll do when someone is watching—and not even realize it.*
Character is built in private. Let your alone time shape who you are in public.

♦ *Don't marry loneliness.*
Loneliness is a feeling, not a person. Wait for purpose, not just companionship.

♦ *Discipline now protects destiny later.*
Saying no to temptation is saying yes to your calling.

♦ *If you want a woman of value, be a man of vision.*
Don't just look for beauty—build a life that matches her purpose.

♦ *Learn to take care of your own heart, your home, and your habits.*
You're practicing for partnership.

♦ *Keep your commitments.*
If your word means something when you're single, it will mean something in marriage.

- *Surround yourself with men who will hold you accountable.*
  You don't need a crowd—you need counsel.

- *Use your single season to serve.*
  Serve God, your church, and others. What you give in this season will bear fruit in the next.

- *Flee youthful lust.*
  Don't play with temptation—run from it. Keep yourself pure until marriage. Your body is a temple, not a playground. Self-control now builds strength for later (see 2 Timothy 2:22).

A Single Man's Prayer

Heavenly Father,
Thank You for this season of singleness. Teach me to walk with wisdom, strength, and purpose. Help me to be whole in You, steady in my faith, and honest in my walk. Let me not be anxious for what's to come, but faithful with what I have. Guard my heart; order my steps, and make me a man after Your own heart. Prepare me not just for a future relationship, but for a life that glorifies You in every stage. In Jesus' name. Amen.

Wisdom Worth Keeping

Wisdom Worth Keeping

_____

_____

_____

_____

_____

_____

_____

_____

_____

_____

_____

_____

_____

_____

_____

_____

_____

_____

_____

_____

_____

_____

_____

_____

Chapter 5

Wisdom for the Married Man

Because Being a Husband Is a Calling, Not Just a Title

Scripture: "Husbands, love your wives, just as Christ loved the church and gave himself up for her" (Ephesians 5:25).

Devotion: Marriage is a daily choice to serve, forgive, and cherish. Let your love mirror Christ's sacrificial love. Small acts of kindness and faithfulness will build a marriage that weathers any storm.

- *Love your wife beyond feelings—love her by decision.*
  Feelings shift, but real love is a choice you make every day.

- *Let love be the glue that holds your relationship together.*
  You're no longer two strands of twine—you are one cord, braided and bound by God.

- *Never lose your identity.*
  A strong marriage is two whole people choosing unity, not one person being swallowed by the other.

- *Be dedicated to each other.*
  Loyalty, respect, and self-sacrifice are not just ideals—they're daily disciplines.

- *Honesty is a foundation.*
  Without truth, trust won't stand. Always be honest, even when it's hard.

- *Give one another breathing room.*
  Togetherness matters, but growth also needs space.

- *Take time to truly know your wife.*
  Don't rush. Don't stall. Keep learning who she is—she's growing, too.

- *Learn the power of patience.*
  Good marriages aren't built in a day. Be willing to wait, work, and water what you planted.

- *Pray often.*
  Pray for her, with her, and over her. When life

shakes marriage, prayer steadies the foundation.

- *Be best friends.*
  Laugh, talk, play, and confide in each other. Your friendship will outlast your youth.

- *Create joy on purpose.*
  Make room for laughter, especially in seasons of trial. A joyful home is resilient.

- *Tell her she's beautiful—often.*
  (Example: "After six decades, I still see a beautiful girl in short shorts on a bicycle.")

- *Make important decisions together.*
  It might seem small to you, but if it matters to her, it ought to matter to you.

- *Choose your words carefully.*
  You can't un-say something. Speak life, not regret.

- *You can't be happy if your wife isn't happy.*
  Her joy is part of your responsibility and reward.

+ *Don't do anything in your wife's absence that you wouldn't do in her presence.*
  Integrity is who you are when no one's watching—but she always matters.

+ *God designed intimacy between a husband and wife to bring life into the world, but He also made it a source of joy.*
  If it felt like hard labor, no one would want to do it. But in His wisdom, He created it to be a gift—one to be cherished within the covenant of marriage.

+ *A moose will fight nearly to the death for the right to mate.*
  If animals will fight for something temporary, how much more should we fight for our relationships and marriages that are meant to last?

A Married Man's Prayer

Heavenly Father,
Thank You for the gift of marriage and the honor of being a husband. Teach me how to love my wife the way Christ loves the church—sacrificially, faithfully, and tenderly. Help me to lead with wisdom,

speak with grace, and protect her heart with honor. Strengthen our bond; restore what's broken and grow what's good. Make our home a place where Your Spirit dwells and Your peace reigns. In Jesus' name. Amen.

Wisdom Worth Keeping

_____
_____
_____
_____
_____
_____
_____
_____
_____
_____
_____
_____
_____
_____
_____
_____
_____
_____
_____
_____
_____
_____
_____
_____

Wisdom Worth Keeping

_____

_____

_____

_____

_____

_____

_____

_____

_____

_____

_____

_____

_____

_____

_____

_____

_____

_____

_____

_____

_____

_____

_____

_____

Chapter 6

Wisdom for the Father

Leading with Love, Strength, and a Godly Example

Scripture: "Fathers, do not provoke your children to anger, but bring them up in the discipline and instruction of the Lord" (Ephesians 6:4).

Devotion: Fatherhood is about shaping souls, not just providing needs. Teach with patience, correct with love, and celebrate your children's growth. Your life is the first Bible they'll read.

- ◆ *Lead by example.*
  Your children may forget what you say, but they'll never forget how you lived.

- ◆ *Don't just try to be a good father—study one.*
  Think of a man you've known a long time who left a strong mark as a father. Don't just guess how he did it. Learn what shaped him and let that wisdom guide you as you leave a path for those coming behind you.

- *Give your children the very best of who you are.*
  Don't just give them what you can buy, but your love, time, attention, and presence.

- *Like a seasoned pilot, know how to fly through the storm.*
  Life won't always be sunny. The winds will come, and the rain will fall. You can't fly over everything—some things you'll have to go through. Learn how to navigate the storm, and let your children see your faith in it.

- *Train your children to obey—not just to follow rules, but to understand responsibility.*
  Teach them early what it means to respect authority and respond with discipline.

- *A switch is not always the answer.*
  Sometimes, correction looks like patience, conversation, or a quiet example. Don't be quick to discipline without first being quick to listen.

- *Teach your children contentment.*
  Help them be grateful for what they have— whether it's little or much. Gratitude is wealth that doesn't run out.

♦ *Make time to talk.*
Don't let work or distractions take away the moments to sit, listen, and speak into their lives. It matters more than you know.

♦ *Apologize when you're wrong.*
It won't make you less of a man in their eyes—it'll make you more of one.

♦ *Pray for your children daily—and pray with them.*
Let them hear you talk to God on their behalf. That kind of covering stays with them forever.

♦ *Let your children face the consequences of their actions.*
Show mercy, yes—but don't always bail them out. Sometimes the best lesson comes through experience. As Proverbs 19:19 says, "A hot-tempered person must pay the penalty; rescue them, and you will have to do it again."

Teach your children responsibility by letting life be the teacher when it needs to be.

A Father's Prayer

Heavenly Father,
Thank You for the gift and responsibility of fatherhood. Help me to lead with love, to guide with wisdom, and to nurture with patience. Teach me to be an example my children can follow, and may my life reflect Your truth and grace. Strengthen me in challenging times, and let Your peace rest over my home. I pray that my children will grow in faith, character, and purpose—walking in the light of Your love. In Jesus' name. Amen.

Wisdom Worth Keeping

_____
_____
_____
_____
_____
_____
_____
_____
_____
_____
_____
_____
_____
_____
_____
_____
_____
_____
_____
_____
_____
_____
_____
_____

Wisdom Worth Keeping

Chapter 7

Wisdom for the Grandfather

Leaving a Legacy of Faith and Wisdom

Scripture: "Children's children are a crown to the aged, and parents are the pride of their children" (Proverbs 17:6).

Devotion: Grandfathering is a second chance to sow seeds of wisdom. Share your stories, offer your prayers, and remind your grandchildren of God's faithfulness. Your influence will echo for generations.

- *Be present.*
  Your presence speaks volumes. Just being there—at games, graduations, or quiet dinners—tells your grandchildren, "You matter to me."

- *Share your stories.*
  Your life experience is a treasure chest. Tell your grandchildren where you came from, what you've learned, and how God brought you through.

◆ *Don't strive for perfection—be consistent.*
A steady hand and calm spirit can be a lighthouse when life gets stormy.

◆ *Listen more than you speak.*
Sometimes just sitting together, letting them talk—or saying nothing at all—communicates more than a sermon.

◆ *Speak life into them.*
Encourage what's good, affirm their gifts, and remind them of who they are in God— before the world tries to tell them otherwise.

◆ *Pray out loud for them.*
Let them hear you call their names in prayer. It will echo in their hearts long after you're gone.

◆ *Live what you teach.*
Show them how a man honors his wife, respects others, keeps his word, and loves Jesus.

◆ *Be the example you wish you had.*
Whether you're continuing a legacy or rewriting one, you have the opportunity to model what a real man looks like.

- *Be patient with their process.*
  They may not "get it" now, but your love, faith, and consistency will speak when they're ready to listen.

- *Invest in their future.*
  Don't just correct bad behavior—pour into their gifts, goals, and growth.

- *Make space for fun.*
  Laughter builds bridges. Don't be afraid to be a little silly—memories are made in the moments that feel light.

- *Teach them responsibility and grace.*
  Hold the standard high, but keep your arms open wide. Discipline with love and always end with encouragement.

- *Be the bridge.*
  Help them connect their past to their future. Knowing their roots gives them the strength to stand taller.

- *Show up spiritually.*
  Let your Bible be worn, your prayers be real, and your faith be visible. Let them see a man

walking with God.

A Grandfather's Prayer

Lord God,

Thank You for the gift of grandchildren and the blessing of another generation to love and guide. Grant me wisdom to lead by example, strength to remain steady, and grace to share the lessons I've learned through the years. May my life speak of Your faithfulness, and may my grandchildren always find safety, encouragement, and truth in my presence. Let me plant seeds that will continue to grow long after I'm gone. In Jesus' name. Amen.

Wisdom Worth Keeping

_____

_____

_____

_____

_____

_____

_____

_____

_____

_____

_____

_____

_____

_____

_____

_____

_____

_____

_____

_____

_____

_____

_____

_____

Wisdom Worth Keeping

Chapter 8

Wisdom for an Unemployed Man

Finding Identity Beyond Work: Trusting God's Provision When Your Calling Feels Bigger Than Your Current Condition

Scripture: "And my God will meet all your needs according to the riches of his glory in Christ Jesus" (Philippians 4:19).

Devotion: Unemployment can feel like loss, but it can also be a season of discovery. Lean on God's provision, use your time wisely, and trust that He is preparing new doors of opportunity.

- *Your worth is not measured by your paycheck, but by your purpose in Christ.*
  A job may end, but your God-given value never changes.

- *A man can just about do anything he puts his mind to—but first, he has to get up.*
  Nothing changes until you decide to rise.

♦ *You can't sleep and do.*
You either rest or move—but you can't succeed doing both at the same time.

♦ *If you put your heart and mind into it, you can do it.*
The mountain may be high, but your determination must be higher.

♦ *Don't wait for the "perfect" job—get busy where you are.*
God blesses movement, not idleness. Use what's in your hand.

♦ *Use this season to build yourself.*
Read, learn, train, and grow. You're not "doing nothing"—you're preparing.

♦ *Keep a schedule—even when you're not working.*
Discipline is a mindset, not just a clock-in time.

♦ *Don't let frustration make you bitter.*
Let it make you better. Bitterness blocks blessings.

- *Surround yourself with wise voices, not just loud ones.*
  Get advice from men who've been down but got back up.

- *Speak life over yourself.*
  Don't let your current status define your future. Your words shape your walk.

- *Trust God with every closed door.*
  Sometimes the job He's preparing you for is bigger than the one you lost.

An Unemployed Man's Prayer

Heavenly Father,
In this season of waiting and searching, I ask for Your strength and direction. Remind me that my value comes from You and not my circumstances. Help me to rise each day with purpose, hope, and discipline. Open doors that no man can shut, and guide my steps into the work You've prepared for me. Provide for my needs and keep my heart from growing weary. In Jesus' name. Amen.

Wisdom Worth Keeping

_____
_____
_____
_____
_____
_____
_____
_____
_____
_____
_____
_____
_____
_____
_____
_____
_____
_____
_____
_____
_____
_____
_____
_____
_____
_____

Wisdom Worth Keeping

Chapter 9

Wisdom for the Working Man

Serving God Faithfully in Your Work: It's More Than a Job—It's a Testimony

Scripture: "Whatever you do, work at it with all your heart, as working for the Lord, not for human masters" (Colossians 3:23).

Devotion: Whether you're punching a clock or running a business, your work is worship. Give your best, stay honest, and remember you represent Christ on the job.

Your labor is more than a job—it's a testimony.

◆ *Work with integrity; your real boss is the Lord.*
Whether anyone sees you or not, God always does. Let your work reflect your faith.

◆ *Work is how we support ourselves and the generations coming after us.*
Your effort today lays the foundation for someone else's tomorrow.

- *Idleness is not a good example for the men walking behind you.*
  Someone is always watching how you carry yourself.

- *Be determined to complete the assignment— no matter how you are treated or how high the odds are stacked against you.*
  A man is proven by what he finishes, not just what he starts.

- *Try to take young men under your wing.*
  Share the best of what you've learned so they can be better than you. Make that your responsibility.

- *Respect your coworkers—even the difficult ones.*
  The test of your character isn't how you treat the easy folks, but how you treat the hard ones.

- *Show up on time, stay consistent, and do your best work.*
  Dependability still matters.

- *Take pride in your craft.*
  Whether you work with your hands, your head, or both—do it well and do it thoroughly.

- *Don't take shortcuts when it comes to your integrity.*
  You may get ahead faster, but you'll never last long that way.

- *Leave work at work.*
  Don't bring the stress home to your wife, your children, or your peace. Learn to separate your load.

- *Thank God for your job—then thank Him for the strength to do it.*
  The ability to work is a blessing many wish they had.

- *Be humble enough to take correction and wise enough to keep learning.*
  A teachable man will always rise.

A Working Man's Prayer

Lord,

Thank You for the strength and opportunity to work. Help me to carry myself with integrity, labor with excellence, and represent You well in every task I take on. Make me a light in my workplace, a mentor to the young, and a steady provider for my family. Remind me that my efforts are not in vain when done for You. Keep my heart pure, my hands diligent, and my mind focused. In Jesus' name. Amen.

Wisdom Worth Keeping

_____

_____

_____

_____

_____

_____

_____

_____

_____

_____

_____

_____

_____

_____

_____

_____

_____

_____

_____

_____

Wisdom Worth Keeping

_____

_____

_____

_____

_____

_____

_____

_____

_____

_____

_____

_____

_____

_____

_____

_____

_____

_____

_____

_____

_____

_____

_____

_____

Chapter 10

Wisdom for the Stressed Man

Finding Peace and Strength in God's Promises:
You Were Never Meant to Carry It All Alone

Scripture: "Cast all your anxiety on him because he cares for you" (1 Peter 5:7).

Devotion: Stress drains, but surrender restores. Take time today to pray, breathe, and release your worries to the One who holds it all together.

♦ *Give God your burdens before they break you.*
Don't wait until you're at the end of your rope—He's been waiting to carry it with you.

♦ *Learn how to be happy, and 99 percent of what you think will become positive.*
Peace doesn't start around you—it starts inside of you.

♦ *Pressure builds power.*
The odd things in life—the things that don't make sense—if you take them the right way,

they'll make you stronger.

- *Let God shape you before life breaks you.*
  If you let the Lord lead, you'll never walk alone.

- *Don't try to outrun your stress—face it, pray through it, and give it a name.*
  You can't fight what you won't face.

- *Remember, rest is not weakness.*
  Even Jesus went away to pray and rest. You can't pour from an empty cup.

- *Everything doesn't need your immediate reaction.*
  Sometimes the wisest thing you can do is be still and quiet.

- *Talk to someone you trust.*
  A real man isn't afraid to say, "I need to talk."

- *Laughter is still good medicine.*
  Find moments to laugh, especially at yourself.

♦ *What you feed your mind will feed your stress or your strength.*
Guard what you watch, listen to, and rehearse in your thoughts.

♦ *Control what you can; release what you can't.*
Don't waste energy on what's outside of your hands—put it in God's.

♦ *Don't bottle things up until they boil over.*
Even a strong pot needs a pressure valve.

♦ *Take life one day at a time.*
God promised grace for *today*. Tomorrow will have its own.

A Stressed Man's Prayer

Heavenly Father,
I come to You worn, but willing. Help me lay my burdens at Your feet and not pick them back up again. Teach me to trust You in the chaos, to breathe when I feel overwhelmed, and to speak peace into my own soul. Strengthen me to keep walking, even when the weight feels heavy. Surround me with wisdom, help, and hope. Let me be a man of calm faith in the middle of every storm. In Jesus' name. Amen.

Wisdom Worth Keeping

_____

_____

_____

_____

_____

_____

_____

_____

_____

_____

_____

_____

_____

_____

_____

_____

_____

_____

_____

_____

_____

_____

_____

_____

_____

Wisdom Worth Keeping

Chapter 11

Wisdom for the Saved Man

Living a Life Set Apart for God's Glory

Scripture: "Therefore, if anyone is in Christ, the new creation has come: The old has gone, the new is here!" (2 Corinthians 5:17).

Devotion: Being saved is more than a moment; it's a lifelong transformation. Walk in the joy of your salvation, and let your life be a light to others.

- *Let your salvation show—not just in what you say, but in how you live.*
  Your life is the loudest sermon you'll ever preach.

- *Loving God will teach you to love people—and yourself.*
  Real salvation doesn't just change your soul; it transforms your actions.

- *Seek the baptism of the Holy Ghost.*
  He is a keeper, a guide, and the power source

for righteous living. You can't do this walk on your own.

♦ *Live a holy and sanctified life.*
Set apart, not perfect—but striving daily to reflect Christ.

♦ *Have faith in God.*
Trust Him through the storms and the sunshine.

♦ *Holiness is still right.*
Even if you don't live it perfectly yet, it's still the standard to reach for, not to settle below (Bishop Charles D. Williams).

♦ *Fear God more than man.*
If you wouldn't do it in front of a person, don't do it before the Lord. When we fear man more than God, we are lost. That shows where our respect really lies.

Remember, the eyes of the Lord are everywhere, watching both the evil and the good. Nothing escapes His notice. His eyes are everywhere, and His standard is what matters most (Bishop Charles D. Williams).

- *Walk humbly before God and others.*
  Salvation is a gift, not a trophy. Let grace guide your attitude. Stay low so God can lift you up.

- *Be a man of prayer*—daily, earnest, and persistent.
  Prayer is the lifeline that keeps your soul connected to Heaven.

- *Guard your heart and mind.*
  What you watch, listen to, and dwell on will either feed your faith or weaken your walk. Don't invite temptation to camp inside your thoughts.

- *Serve with sincerity.*
  Don't do it to be seen—do it because your heart has been changed and is thankful. Saved men serve because they remember what they were saved from.

- *Stand firm when life gets hard.*
  Salvation isn't just about getting saved—it's about *staying* saved. Faithfulness through fire

builds a testimony worth hearing.

♦ *Speak life.*
A saved man doesn't tear others down—he builds, encourages, and points people back to Christ with every word.

♦ *The Bible tells you what to stay out of—and what to get into.*
It's a roadmap for both protection and purpose.

♦ *If God said it, it will work.*
God's Word is not theory—it's proven truth. Stand on it (Bishop Charles D. Williams).

♦ *I've lived long enough to know—I can't find a reason not to love.*
Loving others isn't always easy, but it's always right. I want to love because love is of God, and if God is in me, love ought to come out of me.

♦ *If you can't love me in my dirtiest state, then you don't truly love God in His purest state.*
God didn't wait for us to get cleaned up—He loved us while we were yet sinners. If your

love has conditions, it's not Christlike.

A Saved Man's Prayer

Lord God Almighty,
Thank You for saving me—washing me clean, calling me Your own, and giving me a new start. Help me to live a life that reflects that salvation every day, not in my own strength, but by Your Spirit. Keep me steady when the world shakes, and guard my heart when temptation knocks. Let me fear You more than I fear man, and chase holiness with a sincere heart. Baptize me fresh with the Holy Ghost, and fill me with love that serves, faith that endures, and light that shines in every dark place. May I walk humbly, pray fervently, live righteously, and leave a legacy that points others to You. In Jesus' mighty name. Amen.

Wisdom Worth Keeping

Joe L. Gibbons

Wisdom Worth Keeping

_____
_____
_____
_____
_____
_____
_____
_____
_____
_____
_____
_____
_____
_____
_____
_____
_____
_____
_____
_____
_____
_____
_____
_____
_____

Chapter 12

Wisdom for the Church Man

Serving with Humility and Building
up the Body of Christ

Scripture: "Now you are the body of Christ, and each one of you is a part of it" (1 Corinthians 12:27).

Devotion: The church isn't just a building—it's a body. Your gifts, service, and presence matter. Step up, serve well, and strengthen the family of God.

♦ *Serve your church family with humility and love.*
 Your attitude will set the tone for the spirit of the house. Be the kind of man who brings peace into the room.

♦ *Follow your leader closely—not as if he were God, but as a student.*
 Learn while he's teaching. Ask questions. Watch how he walks. Soak up all the wisdom you can while he's still here. The day will come when you'll wish you had more time with him.

♦ *If you're the pilot, be in the cockpit.*
You can't fly the plane from the backseat.
Take responsibility. Know how to lead, and
when it's your time to pass the baton, make
sure someone else knows the flight plan.

♦ *A church doesn't thrive on its name or building*
It grows because people show up, serve, and
do the right work, faithfully.

♦ *We need the assembly of the saints.*
Get up, get dressed, and *run* to Sunday
school; run to church. It's the spiritual train-
ing ground for your soul.

♦ *Without a walk with God and Sunday school,
you don't have much.*
That foundation will hold you when life
shakes everything else loose.

♦ *Be faithful in the little things.*
Sit in your seat. Volunteer behind the scenes.
Show up when no one else does. God sees
faithfulness, not fanfare.

- *Speak life and encouragement to your church family.*
  A church man builds the body—he doesn't gossip, grumble, or divide it.

- *Use your gifts to serve, not to be seen or for applause.*
  Let God get the glory and help His people grow. Your reward isn't in applause; it's in obedience.

- *Pray often for your pastor, leaders, and church family.*
  The battle is spiritual, and prayer is the front-line defense. Don't let your church fight without you covering them.

- *Remember: the church is not the building—it's the people.*
  Stay connected. Be committed. Don't just show up—*belong.*

- *Be faithful in tithing and giving.*
  There's a blessing in giving. The Lord honors a cheerful giver. When you give from the heart, He returns more than money can buy—peace, favor, and provision in due season.

♦ *If the team can work together, you can't be beaten.* Unity doesn't just win games; it builds legacies.

Prayer for a Church Man

Heavenly Father,

Thank You for calling me to be part of Your church—for placing me in a family of believers to serve and grow with. Thank You for putting me here with purpose. Help me to serve with a humble heart and a willing spirit. Help me to love with sincerity and to follow my leaders with wisdom and grace. Teach me to lead when You call, and to prepare others when my season shifts. Let me be faithful in the small things, steadfast in prayer, and generous in giving. Help me never forget that the church is more than a building—it is a living body. Keep me connected, committed, and Christ-centered. Fill me with Your love, so I may be a blessing to my church family. May my life bring unity, strength, and glory to Your name in this house and beyond. Guide me to always put You first, and to honor You in all I do. In Jesus' mighty name. Amen.

Wisdom Worth Keeping

_____

_____

_____

_____

_____

_____

_____

_____

_____

_____

_____

_____

_____

_____

_____

_____

_____

_____

_____

_____

_____

_____

_____

Wisdom Worth Keeping

Chapter 13

Wisdom for the Preacher

Proclaiming Truth with Boldness and Love

Scripture: "Preach the word; be prepared in season and out of season; correct, rebuke and encourage—with great patience and careful instruction" (2 Timothy 4:2).

Devotion: Preaching is a holy calling, not a performance. Stay faithful to Scripture, speak with love, and let God's Spirit do the changing.

- *Preach the Word, not yourself.*
  The people need Jesus—not your résumé or reputation. Preach so that souls are stirred, not egos.

- *There's room in the kingdom for everybody.*
  There's still hope, even for those the world calls misfits, addicts, or outcasts if they accept Christ. Never count anybody out. God sure didn't count you out.

- *Always be ready to preach.*
  Keep a message in your heart and a Bible in your hand. As Bishop Charles D. Williams used to say, "You never know when you'll be called upon."

- *Don't chase pulpits; chase God.*
  Preaching opportunities will come and go, but the anointing comes from intimacy with the Lord.

- *Study the Word like someone's life depends on it—because it does.*
  Don't just read it to preach; read it to live.

- *Be led by the Spirit, not by emotions or crowds.*
  It's not about volume or style—it's about delivering what thus saith the Lord.

- *Let your life preach louder than your sermons.*
  What you say on Sunday must line up with how you live on Monday.

- *Honor your calling.*
  Whether you preach to five or five thousand, do it with the same fire because it's the same God.

♦ *Don't get jealous of another preacher's gift—celebrate it.*
The kingdom is too big for competition. Your voice has its own assignment.

♦ *Serve your local church faithfully.*
Before you're sent to nations, be faithful sweeping the floor and opening the doors.

♦ *Remember to whom you're accountable.*
Titles don't excuse you from correction. Stay teachable and under godly covering.

♦ *Preach in love, not in pride or bitterness.*
Rebuke if needed—but wrap it in grace, not arrogance.

A Preacher's Prayer

Lord God,
Thank You for the high calling of preaching the gospel. Keep my heart pure, my message sound, and my life in line with Your Word. Help me to preach with clarity, compassion, and conviction. Let me not seek fame or applause, but only to please You. Fill me with the Holy Ghost, guide my study, guard my tongue, and strengthen my walk. May I be a faithful

servant, a humble vessel, and a bold witness for Christ—always ready to speak life, truth, and hope to a dying world. In Jesus' name. Amen.

Joe L. Gibbons

Wisdom Worth Keeping

_____

_____

_____

_____

_____

_____

_____

_____

_____

_____

_____

_____

_____

_____

_____

_____

_____

_____

_____

_____

_____

_____

_____

_____

Wisdom Worth Keeping

Chapter 14

Wisdom for the Retired Man

Embracing a New Season of Purpose and Mentoring

Scripture: "They will still bear fruit in old age, they will stay fresh and green" (Psalm 92:14).

Devotion: Retirement opens the door to new purposes. Invest your time in mentoring, serving, and enjoying the fruit of your labor. You still have much to give.

- ◆ *Retirement is not an end but a redirection.*
  You may have clocked out from the job, but you haven't clocked out from your purpose.

- ◆ *Try to do things that make your life notable.*
  We won't be here forever, but we should leave more than memories behind. Leave a legacy worth talking about.

- ◆ *You're not done growing.*
  Just because you've slowed down doesn't mean you've stopped. Keep learning. Keep

giving. Keep becoming.

♦ *Now is the time to pour into others.*
Share what you've learned—wisdom, fail-
ures, and victories. Young men need your
voice.

♦ *Rest but don't rust.*
Take care of your health, stay active, and stay
involved. Don't sit so long that you forget
how to stand.

♦ *Stay in fellowship.*
Don't disappear from church or community.
We need you. Isolation is the thief of joy.

♦ *You've still got value.*
Don't let the world define your worth by what
you used to do. You are still a man of strength,
wisdom, and dignity.

♦ *Pray even more.*
With fewer distractions, this is your season to
intercede for your family, church, and city.

♦ *Enjoy the fruit of your labor.*
You've worked hard—now take time to laugh, travel, love, and live.

♦ *Leave something behind*—not only money or property—but your faith, example, and good name.

♦ *Be a steady hand in uncertain times.*
When others panic, your calm presence and godly wisdom can be a lighthouse.

A Retired Man's Prayer

Heavenly Father,
Thank You for the seasons of labor, and now this season of reflection, rest, and renewed purpose. Help me to use this time wisely, not simply for leisure, but for legacy. Teach me how to be fruitful, even in my latter years. Open doors for me to mentor, minister, and make a difference. Let my remaining days bring glory to You and peace to my family. Strengthen my body, sharpen my mind, and keep my spirit rooted in You. In Jesus' name. Amen.

Wisdom Worth Keeping

Joe L. Gibbons

Wisdom Worth Keeping

_____
_____
_____
_____
_____
_____
_____
_____
_____
_____
_____
_____
_____
_____
_____
_____
_____
_____
_____
_____
_____
_____
_____

Chapter 15

Wisdom for the Aging Man

Facing Life's Later Years with Grace and Gratitude

Scripture: "Even to your old age and gray hairs I am he, I am he who will sustain you" (Isaiah 46:4).

Devotion: Aging is a gift, not a curse. Let each year deepen your gratitude, and trust that God's hand is steady, even when yours weakens.

- *Grow old with grace, not with grumbling.*
  An aged man ought to reflect wisdom, not weariness. Let your years be your testimony instead of your burden.

- *Ask God to let the life you've lived leave a legacy as valuable to others as it was to you while you walked it.*
  Let what you leave behind point someone else forward.

- *Every aged man should have once followed a wise man.*
  Learn from the paths of those who went before you by spending time together or watching how they lived.

- *Even if your steps have slowed, don't stop stepping.*
  Movement is life, and progress isn't always about speed.

- *Maturity is the crown of the aged.*
  Let your character be seasoned and your spirit settled.

- *Release the past.*
  Let go of what didn't work, what hurt you, and what you couldn't change. Make room for peace.

- *You don't have to speak often, but when you do, let it be filled with grace and truth.*
  The voice of an aged man carries weight—use it wisely.

- *Take care of the vessel God gave you.*
  Respect your body and your health; your usefulness isn't over.

♦ *Remain anchored in the Word.*
The strength of an aged man does not come from youthful energy but from a deep well of faith and devotion.

♦ *Keep your heart open.*
You're never too old to be kind, to learn, or to love again.

♦ *Teach with your walk, not only your words.*
The way you carry yourself in these years may be the greatest lesson you'll ever give.

♦ *Keep the vision of where you've been but learn to live where you are.*
Yesterday shaped you but today is where God is working.

An Aging Man's Prayer

Eternal Father,
I thank You for the journey that has brought me to this point in life. For every scar and every victory, I give You praise. Help me, Lord, to live these years with purpose, humility, and peace. Let the wisdom I've gained be used to uplift others. Make my hands helpful, my heart soft, and my spirit strong. Guide

me as I finish this race with grace, always remember-
ing that as long as I breathe, You still have a purpose
for me. In Jesus' name. Amen.

Wisdom Worth Keeping

_____

_____

_____

_____

_____

_____

_____

_____

_____

_____

_____

_____

_____

_____

_____

_____

_____

_____

_____

_____

_____

_____

_____

_____

_____

_____

Wisdom Worth Keeping

_____

_____

_____

_____

_____

_____

_____

_____

_____

_____

_____

_____

_____

_____

_____

_____

_____

_____

_____

_____

_____

Chapter 16

Wisdom for the Sunday School Superintendent

Teaching the Word and Shaping Generations

Scripture: "Start children off on the way they should go, and even when they are old they will not turn from it" (Proverbs 22:6).

Devotion: Sunday school isn't just a program—it's kingdom work. Whether you teach two or two hundred, sow the Word faithfully, and trust God for the harvest.

- ♦ *Teach with passion; you're shaping eternal lives.*
  This isn't just a classroom—it's kingdom work.

- ♦ *Sunday school is the greatest school in the whole wide world.*
  There'll never be another school that leads a soul to completeness in Christ like Sunday school can.

- *Be on time and be prepared.*
  Your commitment shows the value you place on God's Word and those you're teaching.

- *Healthy, friendly competition between classes for attendance and offering can build excitement.*
  It strengthens unity and helps members feel involved and motivated.

- *Choose teachers who are not only able to teach, but who support the church as a whole.*
  The right team lifts the entire ministry.

- *Start studying the lesson on Monday.*
  Don't wait until Saturday night; treat the lesson as if it matters because it does.

- *Dedicate time each day to reflect and dig into the Word.*
  The more it fills you, the more it will flow from you with power and clarity.

- *Make Sunday school more than just reading—bring it to life.*
  Use visuals, real-life examples, and testimonies. The Word is alive—teach it like it is.

- *Fellowship outside of class builds family.*
  Picnics, game nights, or prayer breakfasts deepen relationships and help lessons to take root.

- *Build a Sunday school people love to attend.*
  When people enjoy being there, they grow. When they grow, they stay. And when they stay, the church has a future.

- *If you build a strong Sunday school today, the church of tomorrow will be rooted and ready.*
  Lay the foundation, brick by brick, lesson by lesson.

A Sunday School Superintendent's Prayer

Lord God,
Thank You for the calling to teach and lead in Sunday school. Help us handle Your Word with care and deliver it with clarity, love, and truth. Give us fresh insight, divine creativity, and a heart for every soul in our classrooms. Bless the students, teachers, and lessons. Let Your Spirit fill every corner of our classes, and may our labor not be in vain. In Jesus' name. Amen.

Wisdom Worth Keeping

Wisdom Worth Keeping

The Wise Journey Forward

A wise man does not just speak wisdom—he lives it, holds onto it, and passes it on. Over the pages of this book, we've explored wisdom for every season of a man's life: from the young man finding his footing, to the father guiding his household, to the elder reflecting on the journey and pointing others toward the path of truth.

These insights are not random thoughts or fleeting reflections—they are time-tested principles forged through prayer, experience, failure, and faith. They have endured storms, celebrated victories, and remained steady in changing times. The heart of this work is not just to offer wisdom, but to encourage the reader to keep it, value it, and live by it.

Proverbs 3:21-22 reminds us, "My son, let not them depart from thine eyes: keep sound wisdom and discretion: So shall they be life unto thy soul, and grace to thy neck." Wisdom is not something to collect and forget. It must be guarded, lived out, and passed on.

Proverbs 4:4-5 instructs, "He taught me also, and said unto me, Let thine heart retain my words: keep my commandments, and live. Get wisdom, get understanding: forget it not; neither decline from the words of my mouth." Wisdom retained becomes a wellspring of life.

The man who finishes well is the one who never stops learning, never stops growing, and never stops listening to God. As you walk away from these pages, may you not just remember the words, but carry them into your relationships, decisions, and destiny.

Ecclesiastes 7:19 declares, "Wisdom strengtheneth the wise more than ten mighty men which are in the city." The strength of a man is not just in his stature or accomplishments, but in his ability to walk with wisdom through every chapter of life.

Proverbs 2:10-11 reminds us, "When wisdom entereth into thine heart, and knowledge is pleasant unto thy soul; Discretion shall preserve thee, understanding shall keep thee." May the words in this book become pleasant to your soul and guidance to your steps.

So, keep learning. Keep walking. Keep sharing. Let this be the beginning of your own legacy of wisdom—lived, preserved, and passed on.

May the Lord bless you and keep you. May He grant you understanding and may the wisdom you've gained here light your path for the years to come.

A Closing Prayer for Wisdom and Understanding

Heavenly Father,
Thank You for the gift of wisdom that comes from You alone. As I come to the end of these pages, I ask that You plant every truth deep within my heart. Help me not just to remember what I've read, but to walk it out daily with courage, humility, and grace. Let Your Holy Spirit guide me in all my ways. Give me discernment to make godly decisions, understanding to lead and serve others well, and strength to stand firm in truth.

Keep me teachable, Lord. Let me be a man who listens more than he speaks, learns more than he boasts, and gives more than he takes. May the wisdom I gain bring honor to You and blessing to those around me.

Preserve my steps with Your truth. Let wisdom enter my heart and shape my thoughts, words, and actions. May understanding guard me in every season of life, and may my life reflect Your glory. In Jesus' name, Amen.

www.ingramcontent.com/pod-product-compliance
Lightning Source LLC
Chambersburg PA
CBHW030923140626
46545CB00016B/2342